MIKULOV

MIK

ULOV

where

houses

sing

ISBN 80-86172-08-2

Dear Readers,

You have just opened a book which in words
and pictures will tell of a town that lies on the
very southern border of our beautiful country,
of a town which is not significant for its size or
number of inhabitants, but still - as you will
learn - has written itself onto the pages of many
chronicles. During its more than eight hundred
years of history, many extraordinary things have
happened here, some of importance far exceeding
the bounderies of our region, our country, and
influencing the course of European history.
Yes, Mikulov has a special magic, loved not only
by its natives, but by many who have only for
a short time immersed themselves in its unique
atmosphere. For those of you who have not had
this opportunity, this book is your sincere invitation
to visit and personally acquaint yourselves with
our lovely town. And for those of us who walk
down its streets daily, and in the hustle of everyday
life have no time to notice the beauty given Mikulov
by Mother Nature and our wise and industrious
ancestors, this book is kind encouragement to
not only preserve that beauty, but increase it with
your considered efforts.

Now, do go forth acquaint yourself with Mikulov's
past and present - first in the pages of this book,
then, if possible, in person. I am sure you will not
regret it.

MUDr. Ivo Koneš
Mayor of Mikulov

A Barbarian in Mikulov

Pavel Šrut

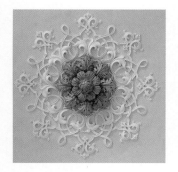  

"...there below the Pálava looms Mount Venus: once it lay like a giant limestone beast across the dreams of Roman legionaires; the people who live there bear a heavy and beautiful yoke."

Jan Skácel

WHERE HOUSES SING

Poets, they say, speak in pictures. Some even write that way. This is known as metaphor. Metaphor is supposed to say more than a direct relation of facts. For example, I say: "Mikulov is a town where singing is often heard". This is reality. You can verify it. But the poet Skácel says: Mikulov is a town where houses sing. That is different. It is a reality which the ordinary visitor to the town cannot easily verify. But it's true, and that's that.

To hear the singing of Mikulov houses, you've got to stalk it, and wait. You have to wait until the singers fall asleep and the houses are alone. You have to stalk the silence, and listen within yourself. This is called contemplation. It is a state where you have your inner field cut and baled, your worries and responsibilities tied in a bundle, and suddenly you get the idea to gather up a few stalks of the happiness you misplaced somewhere else, a long time ago. You can find the secret field in Mikulov, especially when the night is getting on and the air has the color and taste of white wine in a vintner's glass. And then it becomes plain, direct, and you say with the poet: Mikulov is a place where houses sing.

UNDERWATER BELLS

"I used to know an old man who was smarter than I was. Once he taught me how to taste wine. He said: first look through the glass at the sun, and take pleasure in the color. Then, because it pleases you, inhale and smell; enjoy the bouquet. Then flick the glass and put it next to your ear. You hear underwater bells. Then – don't drink. It's not worth the effort. Leave that for the barbarians".

I heard this old-fashioned wisdom from a poet when I was young, back in the sixties. In those days I was worse than a barbarian. I was a smarty-pants from Prague who looked like a sword swallower. I drank only beer, one after the other. One time Skácel invited me to Mikulov; it was my first time. Why did he do it? Now I know: the Moravian poet had decided to civilize a Prague barbarian. It saddened him, this youngster who had never heard the wagons creak over Pálava roads, carrying vats filled with grapes, the sun shining like a golden target in the sky, the air sweet like new wine, and bees and wasps buzzing around the entrance to the cellar...

Under the Holy Hill, which rises exactly as many feet above sea level as there are days in the year, how grateful I have been to him, year after year! And the Holy Hill shines out like a white limestone lighthouse: Mikulov is a shore the sea forgot. And after it flowed away it left a splashing luminosity, and the faraway sound of underwater bells in the summer noontime grapes. Even the real bell in the Church of St. Sebastián on the Holy Hill seems to toll in sweet merciful depths.

WAITING FOR BURČÁK

"Ancient wine presses soberly do their everyday chore above the cellars, on the doorstep the pressed-out grapeskins pile up. The filled-up barrels go down to the secret recesses of the cellar, and the wine boils, really boils, you can hear it with your own ears when you put your head to the oak. They drink a murky brew, wicked and dangerous..."

So Skácel warned. He spoke of Pálava wine, in Mikulov, the town molded by Cardinal Dietrichstein, a man of faith and art, far-seeing, who knew that the Norman cross would have to share its place in the town herald with two curved vintner's knives...

But fie! the wicked and dangerous kind of burčák that floods barbarian Prague in the fall; it is a stupid drink, without a drop of self respect. Avoid this commercial burčák-of-ill-repute! Rather the prayed-for, fussed-over burčák of good education. The burčák sold in Prague, though it may come from Mikulov, is a drink without secrets, like a woman at a nudist beach. Anyway, burčák should not be sold: it's a gift.

I have another bit of wisdom from Mikulov, from the family of Pavel and Dobruška Brichta, a rare and receptive clan. In their house, next to the still-under-renovation Hotel Rohatý Krokodýl, we waited together for burčák.

Waiting for burčák is very similar to waiting for the Easter Bunny. But burčák has no special day set aside for its arrival. You just have to wait, quietly. Sit above the cellar with your eyes half-closed and your ears wide open. No making a ruckus, no yakking, just listen for the burčák's call, until it starts tapping and calling for help like a miner lost in a cave-in. It may be the middle of the night, when the stars are out over Mikulov; it could be the middle of the day, when the sun is shining. But the luckiest time is the morning, when the sun and the stars meet...

THE BLACK MADONNA

The Cardinal who built this town was a visionary, and his patron saint a brown maiden from the Bible who guarded the vineyards. How did this Black Madonna come to reside in shining Mikulov? Read the Bible, all things are found there...

"I am black, but comely, O ye daughters of Jerusalem, Look not upon me, because I am black, because the sun hath looked upon me: my mother's children were angry with me, they made me the keeper of the vineyards; but my own vineyard have I not kept. Tell me, O thou whom my soul loveth, where thou feedest, where thou makest thy flock to rest at noon: for why should I be as one that turneth aside by the flocks of thy companions? Behold, thou art fair, my beloved, yea, pleasant: also our bed is green. The beams of our house are cedar, and our rafters of fir."

The guardian of the vineyard? The Black Madonna of the Song of Solomon was the guardian of love and loving. And this is as it should be.

Work in the vineyard is a heavy and beautiful burden, like love. And the beams of Mikulov houses, though not of cedar but of fir, store up in themselves sunshine and memory, and quiet gathers up in their stonework.

If you want to, I believe that you will see the Mikulov square through the eyes of the poet:

"Renaissance on the square, an old town house with frescoes. In the courtyard is a patio grown over with ivy. Winding stairs. The wind whispers. On a line of hemp the laundry is drying, and a blue brassiere hangs between the sheets".

Which Mikulov Madonna of today does it belong to? asks the barbarian from Prague. Sometimes he gets up early to find out; he might stay up all night long to find the answer. But in the morning... every morning Mikulov is different. And every night the Mikulov houses sing a different song.

The Spiritual Legacy of Cardinal Dietrichstein

Moravia felix - Oh happy Moravia! So many Europeans of other nationalities may have spoken, with poorly-hidden envy, at the turn of the 17th century. Because of its geographical position, it played an important role in the events of the era, economic and military, political and cultural. It lay at the center of European history, and was not only a crossroads, but a bridge between East and West, North and South. In those days Moravia produced the personalities that would determine its fate: Karel Sr. of Žerotín, Karel of Liechtenstein, Albrecht of Valdštejn, and Cardinal Franz Dietrichstein.

These names are symbolic of various directions, opinions, and religious stances. Žerotín and Dietrichstein, it might be said, represented loyalty and steadfastness, Valdštejn and Liechtenstein stood for versatility, change, and conversion. Contemporaries regarded Moravia as an island of religious freedom and tolerance; Moravia at that time hosted twenty different religions and sects. Each had its own followers, its own believers. It could only gain them from the ranks of the established religions by convincing their followers that the „new" belief was better. With peasants and townspeople it was not so much a change of belief as a change of preacher. With the aristocracy it was somewhat more complicated: here acts of conversion were thought out, under various conditions, always with individual reasons, from which politics and career were never very far. Other powerful forces were the attractions of court and Catholic culture, the high standards of Jesuit education, and marriage. As Josef Válka noted in his History of Moravia, the aristocracy of the day did not pass such a strict moral judgement as modern historians do on the converted.

The importance of a strong and unified organization had long been clear. The non-Catholics lacked this unity, which in spite of much effort was never achieved. The Olomouc Bishopric, through the services of the capable bishops Prusinovský, Pavlovský, and Dietrichstein, and the support of the newly-revitalized monasteries as well as newly-arrived orders (Jesuit and Capuchin), firmly stood on the side of Catholic reform; their position also gained strength as many estates passed into Catholic hands. It is estimated that in the mid-16th century only a tenth of Moravian parishes were occupied by the Catholic Church; by 1619 their numbers had reached 300 (of 660 parishes altogether). To this we must add the Evangelist and Anabaptist congregations, but even so Moravia was nearly half-Catholic when the rebellion of the Czech Estates began.

Since 1575 Mikulov had been in the hands of the Dietrichsteins, originally of Carinthia, a family in the service of the Emperor. Maximilian and Sigmund, sons of Adam of Dietrichstein, the founder of the Moravian branch, and their brother Franz, already bound for the church, were firmly rooted in Moravia. Franz was born on September 22, 1570 in Madrid, and through his mother was related to the highest Spanish aristocracy. Their family friendship with the papal nuncio Cardinal Aldobrandini, later Pope Klement VIII, would later have a great effect on his life. František spent his early years first in Mikulov, then at Jesuit schools in Prague and Rome. The Collegium Germanicum, and the later-cannonized Philip Neri, had an important effect on the future Bishop and Cardinal. This high church official, a true prince and ruler, never lost his interest in the people. He became bishop in 1598 through the favor of the papal and imperial courts, despite initial opposition from the chapter house. This favor, however, had its basis in his character and attributes. Though of Moravian origin, he came as a foreigner and had almost no followers to start with. That did not discourage him, rather the opposite.

He was completely devoted to the Church, and to the Baroque „piety of deeds". Before him lay many tasks, secular, political, economic, and administrative. His early days in Moravia were marked by conflicts with Moravian nobleman Karel Sr. of Žerotín, who reminded him of his responsibility to learn the Czech tongue. The Cardinal began to study. As Bishop he needed to communicate with his flock.; he took his priestly and pastoral duties seriously. He visited the entire diocese, including monasteries; he often spoke from the pulpit himself, heard confession (and wrote a published work on confession), visited the sick and imprisoned, and led processions and pilgrimages. Gradually he became an acknowleged representative of Moravia, and after White Mountain, its Governor.

The aftermath of the Battle of White Mountain brought a radical change in the country's religious situation. The current practices of Catholic reform, consisting of patient and unceasing pastoral, educational, and organizational work, were soon replaced by Imperial anti-reform decrees, along with military and administrative pressure. The Cardinal, as Bishop of Olomouc and Governor of Moravia, held state and church power concentrated in his hands, tools he would use to make Moravia a Catholic country.

Mikulov benefited from its position as the center of the estate, and from various powers of obligation held over its subject villages. It was supported by an important and wealthy Jewish community. Mikulov became the Dietrichstein's main residence in 1624, making Mikulov the de facto capital of Moravia. It had a very important printing house, and for a time even a mint.

In 1611 Franz Dietrichstein brought the Capuchin order to Mikulov, for whom in 1623 he built the first Loreta, or Sancta Casa, after the Italian model. The Loreta was named after a place in Italy where the Virgin Mary appeared to a young girl, and became the common name for a shrine where miracles were said to occur, in an era where miracles were needed as a matter of official policy. The Mikulov Loreta would become the model for the one in Prague. Twenty years later the Cardinal invited the Piarist order to Mikulov, establishing the first Piarist school north of the Alps.

Cardinal Dietrichstein confirmed Mikulov in its privileges in 1613, and granted it another weekly market. This was not much use for a town broken and looted during the conflicts of 1619 and 1620. The impoverished country folk, who barely escaped with their lives, had nothing to sell. The Cardinal asked Emperor Ferdinand II for the confiscated estates of Krakovec and Ludmírov, which were granted in 1625; he himself gave Mikulov a large area of nearby forest. That same year he obtained for Mikulov an improvement in its coat-of-arms and a renewal of the right to seal documents with red wax. Red wax was important in an era when illiteracy was widespread, even among minor officials: it meant that a document was of major importance, or came from an important source. The Cardinal's efforts on behalf of the economic prosperity of the town is best deduced from the complaints submitted against his person that the burden of war costs was laid heavily on others, but that his own holdings were spared. So it was until his death in 1636.

Under Cardinal Franz Dietrichstein, the urban development of Mikulov reached its height, and the mostly wooden medieval village became a town built of stone. Dwellings on the square were bought up in 1606, and converted into a town hall; the castle was rebuilt into a modern residential chateau. The Loreta and the Holy Hill became important pilgrimage sites. It was Cardinal Dietrichstein who completed the renovation of the Church of St. Václav, for which he founded a collegiate chapter.

The collegiate chapter is an old and, especially in the past, very important religious institution. Since ancient times, a Bishop had sought the advice and assistance of the priests of his town. St. Eusebius de Vercelli (283-371) and St. Augustine (354-430) endeavored to lead the spiritual community in its social life according to a set of established rules. This way of life was known as the vita canonica (from Latin canon - regulation), and the priests were called canons. The title of the chapter - capitulum - originally meant a place where the canons met daily for prayer and the reading of various parts of their statutes. A collection of these priests was originally called a congregation; after the 3rd Lateran Council in 1179 it was called a chapter. Besides the cathedral chapter at the main church of the Bishop of the diocese, there existed collegiate chapters, established at other important churches. The chapter was made up of dignitaries, who were responsible for maintaining order and discipline in the chapter, and whose way of life was to serve as an example to the other priests, and canons, who were to stand out through exemplary behaviour and education. This was in keeping with the mission of the chapter, which was to see that worship be conducted in a proper way, hold common liturgical hours (a reading of the breviary) in the choir, and assist the Bishop in his work of directing the diocese.

The collegiate chapter at St. Václav Church was founded by Cardinal Dietrichstein on his 55th birthday, September 22, 1625. Permission from Pope Gregory XV was obtained beforehand - the papal bull "Ex debito Pastoralis officii" was issued at St. Peter's in Rome on Jan. 5, 1622. Formal approval by Emperor Ferdinand II came on Feb. 26, 1626.

Mikulov's population now totaled 5,000, up from a mere 500 when the parish was founded. Its patron Karel Dietrichstein-Proskau issued new statutes for the chapter, dated June 30, 1772. The deacon was now to care for the spiritual matters, along with two vicars with no responsibility for religious services; these were the domain of the canon and provost. In 1772 the Mikulov chapter together with those in Brno and Kroměříž requested Rome for permission to exchange their fur cloak for a purple hooded cape, which was approved on March 25, 1774. After 1784, at the order of Emperor Josef II, the provost and canons regained the responsibility for spiritual matters at St. Václav, while the deacons were entrusted with the second Mikulov parish of St. John the Baptist.

The first provost in Mikulov was the knight Jiří Otislav z Kopenic (serving from 1624-1647), who in 1634 gained for himself and his successors the estate at Jiřice u Miroslavi from Cardinal Dietrichstein. As holders of this estate, the Mikulov provosts were considered to be members of the prelacy, with the right to a seat at the Assembly of the Moravian Margrave. After 1848 this right became an empty formality. The Provost was infulled, that is, with the right to carry a miter and staff. The right to wear an insignia around the neck was granted to the chapter by Emperor Franz II on Feb. 8, 1794.

Since the founding of the chapter, 24 provosts and 101 canons have served, many of whom have fulfilled the chapter's motto "Verbo et exemplo", with the subscript "fidei et humanitatis esse ornamentum", that is, to be the ornament of the church and humanity. In other words - to stand out from the others in word and deed, and set an example.

Standing out in the area of church administration was Provost Franz, Count Inzaghi (serving from 1761-1775), a native of Graz, who became Bishop of Trieste in 1775, and Jan Leopold Hay (served 1775-1780), known for his investigation of religious unrest in Wallachia. His activities led to the issue of a decree of tolerance for which, together with a recommendation from Josef Sonnenfels of the Mikulov ghetto (who became his brother-in-law), he was made the Bishop of Hradec Kralové.

• Decisiveness, and the firm determination to pursue a goal, coupled with a certain asceticism and a deep spiritual life: these qualities are apparent in Jiří Sadeler's portrait of Franz Dietrichstein. They helped him to triumph over his intense and explosive character, and served him well in his final reckoning with the rebel Czech nobility after the Battle of White Mountain, which ended in Bohemia with the execution of twenty-seven Czech nobles on June 21, 1621, on the Old Town Square in Prague. At the same time in Moravia, the court under the chairmanship of the Cardinal first confiscated the property of 12 of the dead rebels, later passed death sentences in absentia over 16 nobles who had emigrated, and finally on November 3, 1622, passed death sentences on members of the directorate of the Moravian uprising, as well as other involved knights and townspeople. However, the sentences were commuted to imprisonment, from which the last was set free at the end of the 1620's. On November 19, 1622, the Cardinal issued a general pardon, under which participation in the rebellion was no longer to be punished by death. The confiscation of property was not affected by the pardon; those loyal to the Emperor, as well as Dietrichstein himself, continued to profit by it.

Two other Mikulov provosts excelled during the era of Emperor Josef II. Swiss native Jan Nicholas du Four (1780-1809) was sent as the Austrian advisor and commissioner for spiritual matters to the Austrian Netherlands to pacify the open rebellion which broke out after the religious reforms of Emperor Josef II.

The learned Gregory Norbert Korber served as provost from 1816 to 1843, and was the author of the manuscript of the chapter's annals, and many other writings. Korber's successor Vincenc Weintritt (1843-1849) was professor of religious studies at the philosophy faculty at Vienna University. His lectures were more heartfelt than theologically structured, which attracted the young aristocracy and made him a famous and popular personality. But he fell into disfavor in the matter of Bernard Bolzan, whose works he censored.

Dr. Franz Linke (1934-1944) was saddled with the difficult role of administering the German part of the Brno diocese during the Nazi occupation of Czechoslovakia.

The current Provost (since 1971) is Mons. ThDr. Vladimír Nováček; he was an officer in the Czechoslovak exile army in England, and spent many years in communist prisons and labor camps, then as a construction worker, before becoming the General Vicar of the Brno diocese from 1968 to 1971.

Many of the Mikulov provosts and canons were active in literature and the social sciences, especially theology and history. Many of them published homilies and sermons; their names are today forgotten even by historians, but we might mention Provost Ignáce Xaver Wohlhaupter (1687-1694), author of a book on miracles in the Mikulov Loreta, who also published the text of his sermon for the funeral of Louis Raduit de Souches, victorious defender of Brno against the Swedish. Another significant member of the chapter was biblical scholar and University of Olomouc Professor Tomaš Kestler (1805-1828). Canon Matěj Maria Feyfar (1872-1888), known mainly for his work of history "Die erlauchten Herrn auf Nikolsburg", a broad history of the Liechtenstein and Dietrichstein families, was a member of the Czech Royal Museum in Prague, and also contributed to several Czech theological journals. Let us also mention canon Vojtěch Samec (1967-1995), who was prevented by the prevailing political situation from developing his talents. His genius, stifled by events not of his own making, can be guessed at from his work on the natives of Klobouky, and his study of the remains of St. Cyril and Methodius.

Felix Moravia, Felix Mikulov! Cardinal František Dietrichstein was a complex personality, a product of his times, but the importance and impact of his work far exceed his times. His injunction to the chapter "Verbo et exemplo" - to lead others by word and example - is not only for those few mentioned here. It is a legacy for us all.

• The votive picture in the Mikulov chapel says much about what Cardinal Franz Dietrichstein meant for Mikulov, his beloved town of residence, upon which he left his imprint, both architectural and spiritual.

This "veduta", a symbolic panorama of the town of Mikulov and the Holy Hill, is irreplaceable iconography for anyone who is interested in the history of the town. The chapter is represented by the first canons, headed by Provost Otislav. Cardinal Dietrichstein himself looks up at Mikulov s heavenly protectors, the Black Madonna of the Loreta, and St. Václav, who holds a Baroque Norman shield, decorated with a black eagle, the emblem of the Mikulov chapter.

The shield of the chapter's herald is divided into three fields. In the left upper field is a crowned Virgin Mary clad in white and blue, standing on a half-moon. In her left hand she holds the baby Jesus, and in the right hand a sceptre. Both mother and child have halos. In the upper right field is a figure of St. Václav dressed for battle. Around his neck is a collar, in the right hand a white banner bearing a black eagle; the left hand rests on a Norman shield bearing the same black eagle on a white background. On his head is the princely crown, above the crown a halo. The upper part of the field is gold, the lower red. Two vintner's knives, symbols of the Dietrichsteins, are laid upon the shield.

• The word "chram" (sanctuary) once meant a massive and solid building; it is a word common to all Slovanic languages. It means not only strong walls, but also strength of spirit. The structure is crowned at the highest point by a cross, which stands for victory.

The word "kostel" (church) originally meant fortress. Fortification of churches was forbidden by the Church, but the stone structure itself, surrounded by the walls of the cemetery, stood for sanctuary during difficult times. The church is also the place of meeting between Man and God, God and Man, and Man and Man, between people. The quietness of this place in the middle of the city serves to intensify this atmosphere, and the old tombstones remind us of the meeting which no one escapes. They ask us: Why do you live? What meaning does your life have? What will remain after you?

• After the cathedral in Olomouc, Cardinal Dietrichstein directed his greatest attention to the Church of St. Václav in Mikulov; "because of his special feeling toward this town, he wanted to adorn it with a chapter".

Medieval and Baroque masters of architecture, sculpture, and painting created their works not only to please the eyes and heart, or to praise and honor God according to the wishes of the builder, but also as a means of education and instruction for those who could not understand the Latin spoken at the altar, and could read nothing of their religion in any book, but understood very well the literal and symbolic meaning of the statues and paintings in the church. For example, the pillars in the church nave represent the apostles (and their representatives, the bishops), the outer walls are the knights (the aristocracy), and the floor, those very stones on which one treads, but without which none of this is possible, the simple believers. Many studies have been made of this symbolism.

To understand the meaning of the decoration, indeed the entire church itself, is perhaps more important than to know its architectural history. To know which wall was built when, or how many gold pieces this or that sculpture cost, may be important, but it is not the most important thing to be aware of.

• Řehoř Norbert Korber, the former Premonstrate monk from Louky u Znojma, from 1790 the canon, and eight years later the deacon in Mikulov, became the Mikulov provost in 1816. This broadly-educated man was the author of the handwritten annals of the chapter, as well as many books. It was he who recommended conducting the liturgy in the native language. Although he died in 1843 at the age of 94, he did not live to see the realization of his proposal. He did, however, receive many expressions of disagreement, one of which comes from the pen of another famous man associated with Mikulov, the Piarist Mikuláš Adaukt Voigt.

• The name of provost Karel Landsteiner (who served from 1886 to 1909) is still known today in the history of German literature. He was not only the author of realistic novels and dramas, which did not avoid sensitive social topics, but was also a lyrical poet. He also produced works on science, art history, and theology, and in 1893 a new text of the Passion Play in Hořice na Šumavě, which was used there until 1938. After the Nazi takeover his plays were banned, and their Czech version was not performed until after the events of 1989.

• Dr. Franz Linke became the Mikulov provost in 1934, and after the invasion of the Czech border areas (Sudetenland) in 1938, he was placed at the head of the General Vicarate for the German part of the Brno diocese. As Vicar General he carried all the responsibilities of the post, as well as the de facto powers of a bishop. One of his first tasks was to build a church administration within his territory under the difficult conditions of the Nazi dictatorship, in which he succeeded not only from an organizational standpoint, but in the building of a pastoral center, a financial office, and the care of young people; conditions in the Austrian dioceses served as a model.

• It is difficult, but beautiful to see the roots of tradition, the heritage of our fathers, in the bizzare collection of dusty curiosities assembled by our ancestors over generations, and draw from these roots courage and strength to face life today. Today the halls of the Mikulov provost are peaceful and quiet; the wisdom of the ages breathes upon you, urging you to not only preserve this beauty, but to multiply and pass this treasure on to further generations.

• Members of the Exclusive Collegial Chapter at St. Václav gained in 1794 the right to use medals as an outer sign of their membership in this spiritual organization. Since that time the Provost of the chapter has worn a blue and white ribbon on a purple canon cape carrying the Cross of Leopold, whose blue tines are lined in white, and gilded. In the center is an oval; between the tines of the cross are rays of gold. The decoration is the same on both sides, except for the contents of the oval.

On the front is a red field with a gold relief of Saint Václav carrying a banner and shield; the reverse side shows the herald of the Dietrichsteins, with two hemispheres encircled by a gold lining. The motto reads "Verbo et exemplo"–"Word and example". On the upper tine of the cross is a ring attached to a crown in white and red with gold lining. The crown hangs by a string attached to the neck ribbon. The insigia is attached directly to the ribbon with a ringlet.

• Cardinal Franz Dietrichstein was, as the Bishop of Olomouc, a sovereign lord who for his entire life guarded his independence from Prague. He took care to emphasize that he was not subject to the Margrave of Moravia, as the bishopric was an independent princehood, subject directly to the Czech King. After Olomouc, the bishopric's second official seat was Kroměřiž. He was foremost among the Moravian nobles, and as a wealthy magnate and representative of the aristocracy, he

devoted care to improving his family seat. He was not alone; other examples were the Telč of the Lords of Hradec, the Moravský Krumlov of Pertold z Lipé, Bučovice under the Šemberové, the Liechtenstein's Lednice and Valtice, and especially the Moravská Třebová of Ladislav Velen ze Žerotína. The Dietrichsteins, as owners of Mikulov (and a palace in Brno) had a place of honor among the great families, and as such needed to build a representative seat for the Governor of Moravia.

Mikulov's Holy Hill

The town of Mikulov has three dominant features: the chateau, Kozí vršek (Goat Peak) and its Gothic tower, and the Holy Hill above them. The Holy Hill provides a recognizable backdrop to the town, reinforcing Mikulov's Italian atmosphere.

The hill was long known only as the Tanzenberg, or Dancing Hill, where various unrestrained nighttime revelries would take place every year on the evening before the first of May. After the end of the plague epidemic of 1622, Cardinal Dietrichstein decided to show his gratitude for its passing, and at the same time put an end to the wild carryings-on, by building a chapel on the hilltop. He may have been inspired by North Italian pilgrimage sites such as the famous Sacro Monte at Vares near Milan.

The construction of the Chapel of St. Sebastian was officialy begun on the day of the Visitation of the Virgin Mary, July 2, 1623. A procession led by Cardinal Dietrichstein climbed the hill behind the town to be present at the consecration of the cornerstone. The procession took place regularly after the completion of the new sanctuary, so that in 1626 the Cardinal had a new path built for the pilgrims, lined with shrines representing the Stations of the Cross, which gave people tired out from the steep climb a chance to rest awhile and meditate on the pain and suffering of the Savior, and on His life. A few years later, in 1631, a free-standing bell tower arose near the hilltop chapel; this tower burned down on July 3, 1767.

The structures suffered much from the windborne elements. They were often the target of lightning, especially during summer storms. The Chapel of St. Sebastian caught fire several times, the worst being the fire of 1663. In 1672, Prince Ferdinand Dietrichstein had a bigger church built in its place, which was consecrated in 1679. The central structure is laid out in the shape of a cross, with barrel-vaulted wings and an octagonal cupola. Next to the main altar, consecrated to St. Sebastian, are the altars of St. Roch and St. Karel of Boromej. In 1714 a small sacristy was added behind the main altar. In 1767 the church burned down again, but less than a dozen years later a worse catastrophe befell it: the chapel was closed in the reforms of Emperor Josef II, and its furnishings auctioned off. It was saved from complete destruction only by the fact that it was, together with the entire hill itself, the private property of the Dietrichstein family. Nevertheless, it gradually became a picturesque ruin.

Things finally took a turn for the better in the 1860's. Provost August of Bartenstein, a minor Austrain noble, decided to restore the entire Holy Hill area, including the shrines of the Stations of the Cross. In 1862 he founded a special committee for this purpose, took up a collection, and began repairs. Bartenstein's goal was to restore the Holy Hill as a memorial on the occasion of the 1000th anniversary of the arrival of St. Cyril and St. Methodius, who brought Christianity to Moravia. On August 16, 1863, in the presence of 4000 spectators, the cross was raised on the tower of the restored church; repairs to the interior were subsequently carried out, and the church was reconsecrated on Sept. 8, 1865.

The last serious disaster to occur due to the elements was a stroke of lightning that hit on June 24, 1913. The church caught fire during the Nazi retreat at the end of World War II, on May 5, 1945, but today the white walls of the chapel again shine like a beacon over the countryside.

The history of the smaller sacral structures accompanying the church and bell tower are very interesting. Today there are 16 of them altogether. They were not all installed at the same time, and their present appearance dates from the time of Bartenstein's restoration.

Cardinal Dietrichstein built several shrines with scenes from the Passion along the path leading up the Holy Hill, the first of which was the Farewell of Christ and Mother Mary. This indicates that it was not originally meant to become the Stations of the Cross as we know it. Today's 14 stations are the result of a long development, culminating around the turn of the 18th century. The Passion cycle had varying numbers of "stations", usually seven, evidently because Christ's sufferings were connected with the seven sufferings of the Virgin Mary, and with the seven sins of man - the cause of Christ's death. Seven was probably also the original number of the Mikulov Stations of the Cross, the first of which stands at the foot of the Holy Hill near the former Piarist House, now the House of Writers (Dům spisovatelů).

The original arrangement made clever use of rock outcroppings and small caves. The shrines as they appear today are the product of Bartenstein's modifications. One station in the Passion cycle is the Holy Tomb, rendered in classic Moorish style, today in an unfortunate state of disrepair; it was one of the original shrines, as was the Resurrection, located on a small rise behind the Holy Tomb. Another of the oldest elements of the Passion is the Grieving Virgin Mary, the largest of all the shrines, which stands behind the Church of St. Sebastian on the top of the hill. Nearby is a small, four-sided shrine of uncertain theme, dating from the same era. The tenth station, standing not far from the bell tower, and today lacking any ornamentation, is one of the original structures on the Holy Hill. It dates from the 17th century, and was probably dedicated to St. Barbora.

The remaining shrines on the Holy Hill are newer, and are not part of the Passion cycle. One of them is the shrine of St. Rozálie, protectress from the plague, which is a part of the pilgrimage area, and is located on the other end of the trail atop the Holy Hill near its intersection with the Mikulov road, along with three other shrines found on the slope between the seventh shrine of Christ Bearing the Cross, and the Church of St. Sebastián; one of these was erected in 1675 with funds from an unknown Viennese donor.

The last shrine in the collection was finished in 1776, and on Sept. 1 the entire Way of the Cross was ceremonially consecrated. The fresco in the eighth shrine, depicting Christ's meeting with the women of Jerusalem, is probably a part of the original work. The chapels, restored by the Provost of Bartenstien, were given new paintings of the Way of the Cross by Josef Lebwohl, owner of one of Mikulov's leather factories. The picture on wood of Jesus' third fall, found in the ninth shrine, was probably among these.

The Holy Hill has been drawing pilgrims since 1623. Although the original destination of this pilgrimage was the Black Madonna of the Loreta, worshipers were drawn to the Holy Hill and its Passion scenes. When the Loreta was closed by the reforms of Emperor Josef II, Madonna and its followers were moved to the collegiate church of St. Václav. Since the millennial celebrations of 1865, the Black Madonna has been directly associated with the Holy Hill, for the anniversary of the consecration of St. Sebastián's, Sept. 8, is also the date of the Birth of the Virgin Mary.

The Mikulov pilgrimage never really died out, although it was disapproved of during the totalitarian regime. Even the new Czech settlers who moved to Mikulov after the expulsion of the Sudeten Germans took up the tradition with love and enthusiasm. Unfortunately, the last evidence of their efforts at restoration is the ruined fresco of Christ nailed to the Cross in the eleventh shrine, by Rudolf Gajdoš.

Mikulov's Holy Hill is an extraordinary monument. It is a unique decorative element of this ancient South Moravian town, and says much about the quality of spiritual and cultural life of the community in times past, and present.

• "Black am I, but comely"...The Black Madonna was placed in the first Loreta north of the Alps under the patronage of Cardinal Franz Ditrichstein. It is carried up the hill in October as part of the pilgrimage procession, to gaze out over the town and its vineyards, at the time the grapes are ripening on the vine - the product of an entire year's work by the local people.

• The path of the stations of the cross, of which there were originally seven, begin at the foot of the Holy Hill at the former Piarist house, decorated with a statue of St. Jan Nepomucký in a niche in the wall of the house. The early Baroque symbolism of the stations of the cross spoke clearly to people of that era, even the illiterate. The sculptures date from around 1700, but their themes are from an earlier era. Although they are the work of several unknown artists, together they form a whole. The traditional iconography of Christ is complemented by other figures with more or less negative connotations (floggers, jeering Pharisees, etc.) whose faces show the artist's deep inner appreciation for Christ's pain, and vivid depictions of hate and anger, the sins which brought Christ to the cross.

The first chapel symbolizes the parting of Christ with Mother Mary. The following station shows Christ in his hour of distress in Gethsemene, while the next features the sleeping Apostles and Christ's mute accusation: "Will not one of you stay with me?" The fourth chapel shows Jesus' flogging, the fifth his mocking. In the sixth chapel we see a tormented, seated Christ, and the seventh the carrying of the cross.

• Once a year, on the first Sunday in October, the Holy Hill revives the tradition of the pilgrimage. Boys and girls in traditional costume, children, young and old, all joyfully climb up the hill to take part in the special worship services.

• In 1768, Prince Karel Dietrichstein-Proskau had the largest of the bells melted down after the bell tower on the Holy Hill burned down the preceding year. The new bell, made in Mikulov by Johann Henkelmann, hangs in the tower to this day. It weighs 4300 kg, and takes four strong men to start it swinging. The beautiful tone of the bell carries out over Mikulov and the surrounding countryside, and in good clear weather can be heard 20 km away in Hrušovany nad Jeviškou.

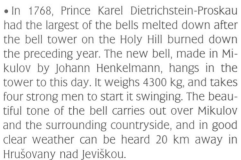

• In 1862 Provost August, Freeman of Barten-stein, decided to restore the Church of St. Sebastian, which was closed in 1786 under the reforms of Emperor Joseph II, and had fallen into disrepair. The plans for its renewal were drawn by Anton Tuter, and carried out by Mikulov builder Josef Langfett. In 1863 the new altar was built, with its painting of the Torture of St. Sebastian by Viennese artist Josef Plank.

The poet Jiří Wolker wrote of the Holy Hill's more famous namesake near Olomouc, but the Holy Hill in Mikulov is still waiting for its poet; its beauty is different, quieter. The white limestone cliffs, covered in the spring by innumerable tiny rare flowers, speak to us of the seeds of pure and peaceful thoughts which grow slowly, modestly, until they bear the fruit of good and noble deeds.

The Town and its Builders

Mikulov - a town with an imposing history amid the poetry of the South Moravian countryside. Over the centuries its builders succeeded in creating a landmark of undeniable elevation and beauty.

Mikulov was the center of a vassal estate whose size changed depending on the political and economic situation of its owners: the Liechtensteins from 1249-1560, and the Dietrichsteins from 1575-1945. Both families were among the leading Moravian aristocracy, cultivating close relations with the ruling courts of the day. Mikulov and its chateau was their main seat, and its buildings, castles, and towers the calling card of its overlords. Its rulers, estate holders who financed the great structures both religious and secular, Jewish and Christian townspeople, vintners and artisans: together they built up a powerful architectural complex, which would fortunately be spared from later waves of destruction and reconstruction. Periods of energetic construction alternated with times of retrenchment that accompanied military conflicts, especially common during the Middle Ages in this border area.

The history of Mikulov was influenced by its location on the Moravian-Austrian border. Since the rise of the Great Moravian Empire in the 9th century, the area below the Pálava had played an important role in the Czech Kingdom's conflicts with its neighbors to the south.

The Mikulov area became part of Moravia after the victory of King Vratislav over the Austrian Babenbergs in 1082. The ancient trade route from the Baltic to the Adriatic crossed the newly-formed border at Mikulov. This peculiar landscape invited settlement, both to guard the Moravian border, and as a market town along the trade route. A log fort on the Chateau Hill served to guard the border between Moravia and Austria in the 11th and 12th centuries.

The first written record of Mikulov dates from 1173, in a document in which Vilém z Pulína and his wife Žofie establish a monastery in Dolní Kounice, and endow it with several villages and patronage rights to various churches, including the one in Mikulov. The document is actually a 14th-century forgery (documents were often forged to reinforce „old" property claims), but seems to accurately document the situation at the end of the 12th century, the existence of the church, and the town itself.

At the beginning of the 13th century, Přemysl Otakar I and his brother, Margrave Jindřich Vladislav, founded a stone castle on the site of the old fortifications, administrated according to another forged document dating from 1218 from the nearby Děvičky Castle by royal burgrave Štěpán z Medlova.

In 1249 Přemysl, Margrave of Moravia, later to become King Přemysl Otakar II, awarded Mikulov to one of his followers, Jindřich of Liechtenstein. This grant was to be part of the colonization of the thinly-settled, economically-underdeveloped, and politically unstable border areas of the Czech Lands.

The heart of the future town was a castle on a limestone outcropping above the village, built around the Church of St. Václav (Wenceslas). The main body of the 13th-century Late Romanesque castle was a square, towered palace. To the south and east of this stood other buildings, of which only fragments remain today, incorporated into the stone foundations and walls of the chateau. There was a cylindrical tower with defensive edge on one side to reflect catapult or cannon fire. Another tower and more living quarters were gradually added, as the castle was always occupied by several families.

In 1362 Mikulov had baths, a magistrate, and butcher's and baker's shops. None of the Gothic town houses of the era survive. They would have been one-storied, wooden, and easy prey to fire, the bane of medieval towns.

The Liechtensteins' acquisition of the Mikulov estate in Moravian territory determined the directional thrust of their politics through succeeding generations. In the unceasing political conflicts between the Moravian and Austrian nobility, they threw their considerable military weight first on one side, then the other, seldom according to principles of loyalty. Jindřich's sons, Jindřich II and Friedrich, fought for Rudolf Hapsburg against Czech King Přemysl Otakar II at the Battle of the Moravian Fields in 1278. In return they were given the right in 1279 to hold a weekly market in Mikulov, greatly contributing to the prosperity of the medieval town. Jan I of Liechtenstein was another master of playing both ends against the middle: he served as castelan for Duke Albrecht III of Austria, who rewarded him an annual market on St. Margaret's Day in 1366, but by 1386, Jan I had become advisor to Czech King Václav IV.

Before the Hussite Wars the Liechtensteins held nine estates, gradually acquired through marriage, reward, purchase, and exchange. The chronicles from 1414 show them owning three estates in Moravia (Mikulov, Drnholec, and Břeclav), and others in Lower Austria. During the Hussite Wars, the Liechtensteins remained firmly in the anti-Hussite camp. Jiří of Liechtenstein, Tridentine Bishop from 1390, actually took part in the arrest of Jan Hus in Constanz. For active assistance rendered to Emperor Zikmund against the Hussites, they gained the nearby town of Podivín, and a tax from the sale of salt in Břeclav, Věstonice, and Drnholec. Emperor Zikmund visited Mikulov several times, and the army of his son-in-law Duke Albrecht had a firm base in there. In 1426, however, the Hussites invaded South Moravia, occupied Břeclav, and burned the town of Mikulov. The Church of St. Václav was burned, and the rapidly-developing town received a blow from which it was long in recovering.

Mikulov was the Liechtensteins' main family seat, always inherited by the oldest member of the family, until 1504, when under Kryštof III the family inheritance was divided into three branches: the Mikulov, the Valtice, and the Styrian. In 1538 the Mikulov estate was further divided between three heirs, the grandsons of Kryštof. In 1560 Mikulov was sold to Ladislav Kereczenyi, who was executed six years later in Belgrade by the Turks. After the death of his son in 1572, leaving no heirs, the Mikulov estate became the property of Emperor Maxmilian II.

The town at the time of its acquisition by the Dietrichstein had at its heart the medieval town square. The fires which struck the inner town in 1536 and 1561 had destroyed the Gothic structures and created space for new Renaissance architecture. On the present site of the town hall stood a brewery, which burned in 1575. On Česká ulice was the old courtyard belonging to the Church of St. Václav. Under the Holy Hill was the Janušův, today Mariánský Mill; another mill stood on the Hnánice Creek in Nové Sady. On the Kozí Peak next to the tower was a salt works which delivered saltpeter to the royal armory in Vienna.

At that time the town had about 2500 residents. Most of the townspeople owned vineyards and gardens. The assortment of artisans answered the needs of a medieval town: there were cobblers, stonecutters, leather workers, brewers, coopers, smiths, bricklayers, cutlers, tailors, fishmongers, wheelwrights, and weavers. There were 9 bread shops and 19 meat shops. The rights of the artisans were protected by their guilds. The cobblers founded their guild in 1476, the tailors in 1571. Tolls were collected at the gates, and were an important source of income for the town. The rules for trading at the market were set down by the town council in 1570, also establishing rules for court cases and guidelines for assessing damages.. The ruling family owned two windmills and a water mill at the Nový Pond, as well as the brewery, the Lord's Court, and a hospital on Videňská Street. Outside the town the Liechtensteins ran a lime quarry and a brick factory. Further development of Mikulov's economy was

• An anonymous contemporary engraving captures Mikulov in the late 16th century. Soldiers climb the western slope toward the castle, which was protected by towers and walls. The Church of St. Václav on the right had no steeple as yet; it was added in 1584.

stimulated by the settlement of the Jews in the 15th century, and the arrival of the Anabaptists in 1524.

By decision of Emperor Maximilian II, Mikulov became the fief of Adam of Dietrichstein (1527-1590), a member of an ancient Austrian noble family. The Mikulov estate became the Dietrichstein's base for their entry into Moravian politics, where they would for centuries play a leading role in the service of the Hapsburg emperors. The two families were bound by ties of personal friendship, and a shared Spanish Catholic cultural background. The first Dietrichstein in Mikulov, Adam was raised at the court of Ferdinand I in Madrid, becoming a friend and advisor to Maximilian II. In 1562 he helped to arrange the election of Maximilian II as Holy Roman Emperor, and the coronation of Rudolf II in Hungary in 1572. He became high chamberlain after Rudolf's move to Prague; it is indicative of his position that Maximilian II chose to sell the hereditary rights to Mikulov to him in particular. An agile politician, Adam of Dietrichstein began to set the economically devastated estate back on its feet. In 1577 he gained another annual market day for the town, and two years later the right to seal official documents with red wax, a signal to often-illiterate officials and couriers that a document was of high importance.

Adam's successor would become a towering figure in 17th century Moravian history: Cardinal Franz Dietrichstein (1570-1636), Bishop of Olomouc, and Governor of Moravia after the Battle of White Mountain. Under his rule the provincial border town of Mikulov became the de facto capital of Moravia. After taking charge of the estate in 1611, he systematically transformed the town into a residence worthy of his powerful standing. His first clerical act in office was to invite the Capuchin Order to Mikulov, building for them the Monastery of St. Francis inside the northeast corner of the city walls. It was consecrated on August 22, 1613; construction of a Loreta church nearby was begun in 1623.

The orientation of the Renaissance aristocrat Cardianal Dietrichstein towards Italian culture determined his choice of architects for his building projects, and gave a new face to the town of Mikulov. The overall impression of the Late Renaissance complex of buildings on the square was amplified in 1623-1626 by the construction of the Chapel of St. Sebastian on the top of the Holy Hill, and the shrines on the hillside along the trail up the steep slope. His good taste, and the desire to leave something behind, led him to endow the town with gifts of lasting value, a unique blending of village and countryside, the town rising out of the fields in an imposing silhouette.

During the time of the Thirty Years War, when the economy of the Czech Lands broke down under the burden of military conflict, the town of Mikulov grew all the more, thanks to the Cardinal's political position, adding other institutions and buildings. When the Piarist Order came to Mikulov in 1631, it was given a complex of buildings built in 1401 at the edge of town, formerly housing a hospital and its chapel. The town's center was surrounded by new stone walls. The Church of St. Václav was enlarged and renovated, and nearby a new provost's house was added.

Through the years 1611-1644 the Cardinal rebuilt the sober medieval castle into a Renaissance chateau. The four corner bastions became residential halls. The original Gothic main bastion on the north side became the main chateau court, the Hall of Ancestors. The wings of the south court were joined by an elevated arcade, to spare the finely-clad residents and servants of the castle from having to walk across the often-muddy chateau courtyard, and a south wing was built in front of the castle walls on the south side. A new theater was built, and a new main entrance was designed. The long medieval approach, from the east around the south slope to the western wall and its Gothic bastions, had lost its military usefulness. It was replaced by a direct entrance from the east above the Church of St. Václav, which survives in the northern part of the Temné (Dark) Gate. A park with Mediterranian trees and shrubs was introduced below the chateau.

To his successor Maximilian (1636-1655) the Cardinal left a beautified town with a splendid palace, and new spiritual and educational institutions a dignified seat for the holder of the Mikulov estate. The economic situation of the town after the Thirty Years War was improved with the renewal of the town's privileges, and subsidies to support the production and trade of wine. A decline in demand for wine led to a buildup in the inventories of the chateau's cellars; for this the Prince ordered a gigantic barrel with a volume of 1,010 hl, which survives to this day.

The town came onto hard times after the defeat of the Austrian army at the Battle of Jankov in 1645, when Mikulov was invaded and occupied by Swedish soldiers. The Swedes carried off 54 cannon, 1200 cannonballs, and the Cardinal's rare library, gained mainly through confiscation of the libraries of non-Catholics, which they hauled back to Queen Christina in 48 barrels. The devastating year-long occupation ended April 2, 1646 with the night attack led by Raduit de Souches. Hunger and famine were the results of the Swedish invasion, along with a decline in population and the ruination of the town's economy. But Mikulov would soon recover from these injuries.

Maximilian's son Ferdinand II, Imperial Chamberlain, High Chancellor of Moravia, and the province's hejtman (administrator), ruled the estate from 1655 to 1689. His reign was marked by wars with Turkey and Hungary, which reached as far as South Moravia. In 1663 the army of the Transylvanian Prince Rakoczi raided the area around Mikulov. After the war a quarter of the houses in the town were uninhabited, and a fifth of the vineyards left untended. The Prince made efforts to improve matters with the help of the guilds, and to support trade permitted a sixth market day, to fall on the Sunday after St. Václav's Day. These measures evidently helped, as seen from the renovations on the chateau and a new wave of construction in the town in the late 17th century.

On the third chateau courtyard a ball court was built, the Temná Gate was rebuilt, a terrace before the eastern wing of the south palace (1682), and an orangery below that (1686). The Piarist Chruch of St. John the Baptist was enlarged. Near the Valtice Gate a hospital was built, serving as a poorhouse for 33 people. In the 1660's the construction of a hospital was undertaken on the Kamenný řádek, part of which was the Chapel of the Virgin Mary Assisting, a simple Baroque structure with a relief of St. Mary and the herald of the Dietrichsteins, the work of Ignáce Lengelacher.

Ferdinand's oldest son Leopold, an extravagant Baroque aristocrat with impeccable taste, administered the estate in 1698-1708. He hired architects of the highest reputation: John Bernard Fischer von Erlach, Lucas Hildebrandt, and the Viennese builders Jean Trehet and Kristián Alexander Oedetl. The chateau's fortifications and the town wall were strengthened. A barracks for the chateau guard was built, a stable near the western bastion, and new luxury quarters above the eastern terrace. The account books record payments to bricklayers and painters, roofers and locksmiths, stucco artists, gilders, and stonecutters. Furniture was bought, and paintings, along with 4000 nails to hang them up with! Painters of frescoes and glass were hired, and sculptors from Austria and Italy. Also appearing in the accounts are payments for musical instruments for the chapel, and for the showing of an Italian comedy.

Unfortunately, the income from Leopold's estate did not cover the cost of the projects. After his death his brother Walter Xaver (1664-1738), until then a church functionary in Olomouc, took over the family property. The desperate financial situation was made worse by a terrible fire on August 10, 1719, which broke out in the Jewish Quarter and spread to the chateau. A pile of ruins was all that remained of the luxurious residence. The frugal Walter called on the previous builders to restore the building, but without the costly artistic ambitions of Kristián Oedetl. The original three-story building was reduced to two stories. A sala terrena was installed in the southern area, and above it a terrace, still in the spirit of Leopold's extravagance. A new terrace was built above the gate to the first courtyard alongside the Hall of Ancestors, and the hall was joined with a stairway to the original Baroque theater, renovated in 1727 as a library. The foyer to the Hall of Ancestors gained a new stairway, with iron bars designed by Brno architect Heinrich Gottfried Förster, and small sculptures by Ignác Lengelacher. The role of artistic advisor was entrusted to Antonín Josef Prenner, painter of the murals in the sala terrena. What the chateau lacked in elegance, these then lesser-known artists made up for in originality. This was especially true of Lengelacher, making his debut as a young sculptor in Moravia. His work can be found in almost all of the churches and villages in the Mikulov area. Ignác Lengelacher made his name with his work at the Mikulov estate, and became South Moravia's most important Baroque sculptor.

• Adam of Dietrichstein (1527-1590) was the High Chamberlain for Empress Marie and her son Rudolf II. He was the ambassador of the Austrian court in Madrid during the time spent by the Emperor's sons Rudlof and Arnošt with the Spanish Hapsburgs in 1563-1571. His connections with the ruling court were strengthened by his marriage to Markéta of Cordona, daughter of the governor of Sardinia and a relative of the Hapsburgs who was related to the King of Aragon.

The building of a road, from Vienna through Mikulov and Pohořelice to Brno, aided the growth of trade. The leading Nuremburg trading companies set up branches in Mikulov, trading in sugar, coffee, exotic spices, and indigo. Relative freedom of exchange - seven annual markets, each lasting four weeks - put the town at the forefront of trade in Moravia, giving Mikulov residents the wherewithal to build.

In the years 1738-1782 the estate was managed by Prince Karel Maximilian, one of the most educated courtiers of Maria Theresa. He employed Moravian architect František Antonín Grimm, who designed stables on the second courtyard, a terrace for the summer riding hall, and some smaller outbuildings in and around the town.

Prince Jan Karel Dietrichstein, who ruled from 1782 to 1806, served as the Austrian ambassador to Denmark, to Fredrick II in Berlin, and in Venice. During his long absences, the Mikulov estate was managed by his formidable wife, Marie Kristyna.

On Sept. 14, 1784, a fire broke out in the kitchen of the financial offices next to the canon houses, drastically changing the look of the town square. The neighboring post office burned, as well as the town hall, the Capuchin church, monastery, and the Church of St. Anne. After this catastrophe the Prince's court moved to Vienna permanently. The devastated square and deserted chateau, without the lord, his guests and servants - this was Mikulov at the end of the 18th century.

With the Napoleonic Wars, Mikulov found itself the scene of great historic events. In December 1798 the Russian Army under General Suvorov passed through, and after Napoleon's victory at Ulm, the French Army on its way to Brno. After the Battle of Austerlitz in December 1805, peace talks were held at the Mikulov chateau, led by Talleyrand on the French side, and Prince Liechtenstein for the Austrians. On the morning of December 12, Napoleon himself appeared, accompanied by Marshals Murat, Soult, Berthier, and Bernadotte, the last of whom would one day become the King of Sweden. They were greeted by the Dietrichstein Guard and artillery. Columns of captured Russian and Austrian soldiers marched by, followed by the victorious French. With them came typhus. The peace talks were moved to Bratislava. A hospital for wounded captured soldiers was set up on the ground floor of the chateau, and in the Piarist school for the French. A wooden cross used to stand by the road to Drasenhofen to mark a cemetery for French victims of the epidemic.

The chateau's new owner, František Josef Dietrichstein (ruled 1806-1854), persuaded by Tsar Alexander I to fight against Napoleon, called on his serfs to join the militia. After the Battle of Wargram in 1809 the French again occupied Mikulov. War requisitions forced the Prince to sell estates at Židlochovice and Hrušovany, and farms at Velké Němčice and Prštice to the Count of Saxony-Těšín.

Mikulov again saw the famous personages of history after the fall of Napoleon, when Tsar Alexander of Russia and King Freidrich of Prussia travelled through on the way to the Congress of Vienna, which was to redraw the map of Europe.

• In 1447 Perchta of Rožmberk married Jan of Liechtenstein, the owner of Mikulov. This political marriage with a robber knight lasted nearly thirty years before Perchta fled to Vienna. Her life in Mikulov with a rough-hewn husband and cruel mother-in-law is described in her letters to relatives, which are the basis for the legend of the White Lady, said to haunt the Rožmberk's Czech castles. In Mikulov her legend has been nearly forgotten.

At the end of the 18th century Mikulov had 7,440 inhabitants living in 591 houses; of these 4,420 in the Christian town, and 3,020 in 169 houses in the Jewish area, which made it the fifth largest town in Moravia. In 1754 Bernard Goldschmied opened the first wholesale business in Mikulov. By the end of the century several others opened, dealing in Austrian and Hungarian wool, iron goods, and wine. There were temporary warehouses for goods traded between Austria and Hungary in the south, and Moravian, Silesian, and Polish cities in the north. Business was dominated by the Jewish community.

Mikulov, devastated by marching armies at the beginning of the century, suffered still further from fires. In 1800 Česká Street burned, along with adjacent parts of Kamenný řádek and the Upper Village, today's Pavlovská ulice, which burned again in 1832. The old quarter where Anabaptists lived in the 16th century lay in ashes a year later

Franz Josef Dietrichstein was the last of the builder princes of Mikulov. In 1827-28 he built the Empire house on the courtyard for the office which assessed and collected taxes from peasants and renters on the nobility's lands. A new carriage road ran from the gate on the square (built in 1839), through the courtyard and the park, to the Smoke Tower. The chateau chapel and the roof of the main steeple were renovated by Viennese architect Heinrich Koch. Koch also designed the reconstruction of the Church of the Loreta, which burned in 1784, and was transformed in 1845-1852 into the Dietrichstein Tomb.

In 1866, a half century after the peace talks with Napoleon, Mikulov again found itself at the center of events. After the defeat of Austria at Hradec Králové in the Austro-Prussian War, the Austrian army retreated through Mikulov, pursued by the Prussians. The headquarters of the Prussian army, along with King Wilhelm I, arrived in Mikulov for peace talks with Austrian representatives. After heated discussions, a tentative peace was signed on July 26. The result of this agreement was a redivision of the power arrangements between the German states and Austria, setting up conditions that would later bring on World War I. The invasion of soldiers brought war requisitions and cholera, which killed 231 Mikulov residents and 244 Prussian soldiers.

The early 19th century was the last period of strong economic development in Mikulov, broken by the building of the railroad, the new transportation link between Vienna and Brno. The railroad line was built through Břeclav, bypassing Mikulov. The Brno-Vienna highway could not compete, and Mikulov's residents gradually dwindled away, mainly to Vienna.

The twentieth century's two world wars left their mark on Mikulov. On October 8, 1938 the town was occupied and annexed to the German Reich. Part of the Czech population was forced to leave, and most of its remaining Jewish inhabitants became victims of the Holocaust. After the German-speaking population was deported, Mikulov was temporarily deserted. Its new inhabitants initiated the reconstruction of the chateau complex, which had burned to the ground on April 22. 1945 during the fighting. Reconstruction of the chateau was directed by Brno architect Otakar Oplatek.

Mikulov's location on the closed border, away from the main railroad line, turned it for fifty years into a stagnating border village. The opening of the border in 1989 again brought change. Mikulov's protected status as an urban monument reserve has meant the gradual renewal of the charm it was given by its builders.

• The medieval castle of the Liechtensteins is hidden within the walls of today's Baroque chateau. The Romanesque core of the main chateau tower is the work of Czech builders from before 1218. Into it was set he octagonal Chapel of the Virgin Mary and St. John the Evangelist in 1380. The rocky entrance to the main courtyard, with its Gothic well, is bridged by a portal from the turn of the 14th century. The original Gothic castle keep was incorporated into the massive northern bastion of the southern castle in the 17th century, and now houses the Hall of Ancestors. The Edge Tower was built in the 13th and 14th centuries. It has three levels, with crenellations on the top. Next to it was a gate which closed off the approach to the second courtyard from the outer area north of the castle. In the mid-1400's a palace was built on the eastern walls of the second courtyard, connected to the southern castle by a five-sided corner tower next to the chapel. The castle had a fortified access road guarding the approach to the castle around the towers on the courtyard and the Edge Tower, with the rocky tunnel gate leading into the south castle.

The three-quarter-circle tower was built at the western entrance to the second courtyard in the mid-16th century during the Gothic-Renaissance reconstruction of the castle.

• Part of a limestone relief of a scene from the Last Judgment is found in the collection of the Regional Museum. This Early Gothic rendition and the place it was found indicate its origin as a tympanum from the old hospital chapel, established in 1401 at the cemetery below the castle.

• The chateau's art collection suffered greatly from the wars. During the Second World War a cycle of Gothic wooden paintings of the Sufferings of Christ was lost. This picture of Christ wearing the Crown of Thorns is perhaps a part of this lost cycle.

Brünner Thor

• The Turkish raids on Moravia in the early 16th century and the development of gunpowder required reinforcement of Mikulov's fortifications. The function of the defensive towers on the southern court were taken over c. 1560 by four bastions on the rocks above the cliffs. The castle became a star-shaped fortress, protected against cannon fire from below. The eastern palace was closed off on the second court by a bastion aligned with the gates by the Edge Tower. The castle's defenses were given further reinforcement against possible long-range fire from the newly-built Powder

Tower on the Kozí Peak opposite the castle.

After 1625 the town was surrounded by stone walls, reinforced in 1703. It was a simple, two-meter thick wall with a water-filled moat. In the north it joined a tower of the chateau; behind the church it was broken by the Brno Gate. It copied the line of the square along Česká street, at the Capuchin monastery it turned south, strengthened with small bastions. The southern walls led up to the Vienna Gate, and ended at the walls of the chateau. Mikulov's gates were torn down in 1836.

• The Renaissance house U rytířů was built after the town's fire in 1561 by converting several Gothic houses. The corner protrusion with an onion dome top was created by walling up the Gothic corner turret. A passage led through the main facade to the courtyard, and the residential level with its wooden ceilings. The courtyard was also accessible via a side gate. On the side toward the chateau was a one-winged building with arcades on the first floor, which led to an arcaded stairway. The original two-story house was raised by one story during the 19th century. A very fine, and for Mikulov unique, work of sgraffiti on the outer facade and the courtyard, depicting scenes from contemporary life and from the Old Testament, underlines the uniqueness of this exceptional building.

• Maximilian I, King of Germany and Holy Roman Emperor, master organizer of dynastic weddings, embodied the slogan: "Let others fight wars, you, happy Austria, marry!" He arranged the marriage of his son with the heiress to the Spanish throne. For his grandchildren Ferdinand and Marie he set up a double wedding with the children of Vladislav Jagellonský, Anna and Ludvík, in 1515. The politics of marriage bore rich fruit. Ludvík Jagellonský died at the Battle of Mohač in 1526, and the Czech throne fell to his brother-in-law Ferdinand Hapsburg.

Zíkmund Dietrichstein served as ambassador between the Hapsburg and Jagellonský families during marriage negotiations. The Emperor showed his gratitude by accompanying the wedding of Zíkmund and his bride Barbora z Rotálu on the same day the royal children married, July 22, 1515. Shown here is Dietrichstein's wedding celebration, with the royal newlyweds occupying places of honor. Their costumes were designed by Albrecht Dürer.

• Opposite is the chateau's four-story Renaissance tower, topped with an arcaded gallery and toscan columns below an onion dome with lantern bay. Its Romanesque predecessor, mentioned in the first written record of Mikulov, was burned in 1426 by the Hussites. A new church was built in the town, but it burned down in 1584. The new Gothic church was built by the St. Jacob's Church building workshop in Brno. Surviving from this era are the presbytery with ribbed, net, and star vaulting, with three naves and tower with a sacristy. During the Mannerist reconstruction of 1625-1640 the triumphal arch was changed, the windows lost their Gothic crosses, and the sacristy entrance was modified. Openings were made for the musicians' balcony and the town's oratory. Under Cardinal Dietrichstein the triple nave was extended with a lord's oratory for the ruling nobity, accessible from an elevated walkway leading from the chateau. The triple nave was given Manneristic cross vaulting and stucco decoration. At the same time a new provost's house was built.

At the beginning of the 18th century, artist Ignác Lengelacher gave the church its altar and Pieta. In the mid-18th century Brno sculptor Ondřej Schweigl gave the church its furnishings and altar sculptures. The pictures around the altar are by Mikulov native Josef Adolph.

• A silver goblet inlaid with coins; on the bottom of the inside is a medallion with a portrait of Jan Hus. It probably belonged to the 16th century Protestant congregation that worshiped at today's St. John the Baptist.

• This remnant of a silver chain with semi-precious stones and figure of joined hands is an example of the beauty of Renaissance jewelry.

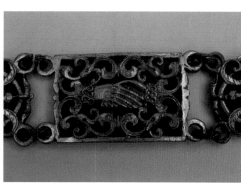

•During the Renaissance, wooden painted ceilings adorned the homes of wealthy townspeople. Few of them survive today. Hence the exceptional value of the ceiling in the townhouse on Na Jamě Street, uncovered and restored in the 1920's.

• Fish farming was a lucrative branch of the Leichtenstein's Mikulov economy; in the mid-16th century it accounted for 44 % of the income of the estate, while the brewery was responsible for 20 %, tolls 11 %, with sales of wood and wine bringing less.

The Leichtensteins began building fish ponds before the Hussite Wars. In 1418 they bought the land of the Sedlec pond, which fell to the Lednice part of the property when the family holdings were divided in 1565. Two large fish ponds, the Šibeniční and the Nový, remained, along with seven small ones on the Mušlov creek: Držkař, Leluš, Střelecký, Klapač, Kněžský, Starohorský, and Turzes. By 1574 a mill stood by the pond near the Valtice road.

There was an island at the center of the Nový fishpond. An ornamental orchard was planted there in the early 1600's, with a "summer house and various artistic creations", according to the chronicles from 1629. The pond lay on the border creek, through whose center ran the provincial border. Long disputes were maintained over the rights to its use, until 1826 when it was awarded to the Moravian side. Part of the pond was drained in 1859 to allow passage of the railway.

The small chateau on the island was a destination for the nobility's outings. Its kitchen was richly equipped with Anabaptist pottery. After WWII the chateau deteriorated; only ruins remain today.

• The Capuchin monastery owned three one-story houses, built after 1625 for the canons of the chapter of St. Václav, and a bigger house opposite, with the sacristy for the Loreta and storage for gifts donated to the Black Madonna of the Loreta. The whole collection of buildings formed a little square for pilgrims to the Loreta adjacent to the town marketplace, with an entrance onto the square. After arriving in the town pilgrims could repair to one of nine small houses built for them by the Cardinal near the south wall.

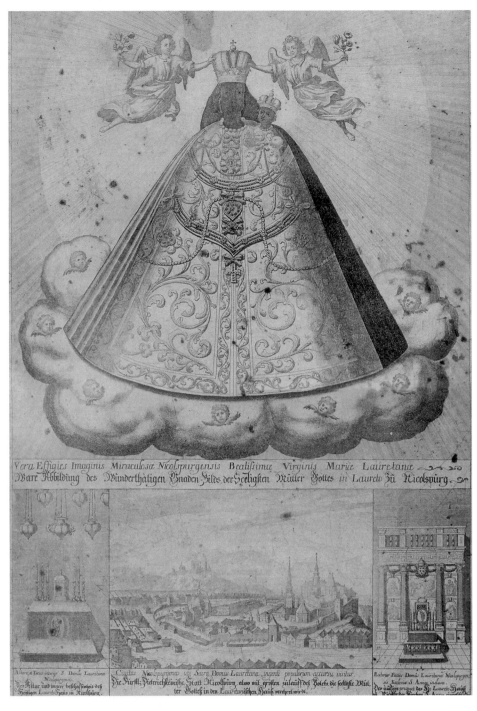

• In 1673 Mikulov canon Ignác Xaver Wohl-haupter published a brochure on miracles that had taken place in the Loreta. This engraving shows the state of the chateau after it was completed in the panorama in the lower part of the engraving, which depicts the town after the building and modifications of the 17th century. The etching is dominated by a wooden sculpture of Mother Mary and child, today installed in the Church of St. Václav. The Sancta Casa, or Loreta, was built out of doors. The church around it, consecrated to St. Anne, was built by the Cardinal's successor Maximilian Dietrichstein. The overall design was created by Italian architect Giovanni Giacomo Tencalla, and it was completed in 1656. The etching indicates that the Sancta Casa in Mikulov was intended to be a copy of that of the Bramant Chapel, built in 1510 at the Italian Loreta.

The view depicts the town from the Brno Gate, set into the walls surrounding the town center. The former Tanzenburg, by then renamed as the Holy Hill, is crowned with the Chapel of St. Sebastian, the bell tower, and the shrines. The castle has become a chateau after the Late Renaissance renovation. The left, eastern corner of the walls is built up with canon houses, the Capuchin monastery, and the Church of St. Anne with its towers. The one-story building next to St. Anne's, joined to it at a right angle, was built in 1652 as a sacristy for the church and the jewelry belonging to the Loreta's Madonna. The treasure of the Loreta, stored in various chests, consisted of the Madonna's wardrobe and gold jewelry. The square is closed off on the south side by the Vienna Gate.

• On Sept. 14, 1784, one of the most destructive fires in the history of the town broke out in the vicinity of the canon houses. That day the entire northern side of the square burned down, together with the Loreta church and the Capuchin monastery. Three hundred and fifty houses were destroyed. The monastery ceased to exist, and the Loreta Church of St. Anne remained a ruin until 1845. At the end of the 18th century its stone front wall was to have been sold off as building material.

• The stone facade of the former Loreta church, dating from 1700, has become one of the town's artistic monuments. Its designer, Viennese architect Jan Bernard Fischer von Erlach, here brings his expression of Roman monumental Baroque to perfection. The reconstruction of the Loreta church was commissioned by Leopold Dietrichstein. He had the original single-towered facade razed, and replaced by a front with two towers, probably meant to be the beginning of an overall reconstruction of the church.

• Prince Franz Josef Dietrichstein deserves credit for saving the remnants of the burned-out Loreta church and transforming it into the Dietrichstein mausoleum. The Dietrichstein dead had been buried in the Loreta church since the late 17th century. The present sacristy served as the funeral chapel. After the fire in 1784 the rescued coffins were placed in the Church of St. Václav.

The reconstruction of the Loreta was carried out in 1845-1852 by architect Heinrich Koch. The presbytery became a funeral chapel with Empire facade. The collapsed vault of the nave was not rebuilt, and its area became a courtyard. The side chapels became halls in which lie 45 coffins holding the remains of members of the Dietrichstein family, and in 1852 ceremonially reinterred, laid on new pedestals. The front of the church was decorated with statues of a standing Christ and two angels, the work of Josef Kässmann. The onion domes on the towers dating from the early 18th century were not rebuilt. The statue of Prince Franz Josef, done in 1859 by Emanuel Max for the Hall of Ancestors in the Mikulov chateau, was moved to the courtyard.

• The Loreta's Church of St. Anne has a complex history. Only the presbytery and its neighboring chapel, roofed by a so-called Náchod copula with lantern bay remained by the mid-1600's. The architectural design of Giovanni Giacoma Tencalla was complemented by the Manneristic stuccos of his brother, Giovanni Tencalla (yes, the brothers had the same Christian name).

• The sacristy of the Loreta church from 1679 still features a Manneristic stucco ornamentation, created by Vienna artist Giovanni Castelli. The much-deteriorated, and almost one-third destroyed stucco was restored during the reconstruction of the canon houses in the 1970's. The space is used today as a municipal exhibition hall.

• This 1826 plan of Mikulov still allows one to orient oneself in the town, and gives an idea of its development since medieval times.

The market town of Mikulov was conceived and founded along the trade route to Laa an der Thaya during the colonization of the Czech border areas in the 13th century.

The trail to the north had led through here since ancient times, across a ford over the River Dyje at Mušov; from the saddle over Goat Peak and the Chateau Hill the road led into the old Slavonic village at the site of today's Česká Street and the area around the Church of St. Václav. From there the road led across a ford over the Hnánice Creek, the only watercourse in the town, to the foot of the Holy Hill. There it turned sharply to the south along its western slope, leading in the direction of Břeclav and Vienna. Another road led from the northeast, joining the Vienna road at the church, skirting the Chateau Hill, and off to the south, to Laa an der Thaya.

The Liechtenstein chronicles from 1414 refer to the old market village of Mikulov as a town, and enable us to reconstruct its medieval appearance as a fortified border town. The northern entrance to the town was near the Church of St. Václav. To the southeast, on the site of today's Piarist school, stood the Valtice gate; to the southwest, on the right bank of the Hnánice, was the Laa Gate. The town was laid out in the shape of a triangle with its peak to the north, where there was a spacious marketplace; in the southern, wider part lay the Livestock Market. After the mid-14th century the inner town and its 37 houses were surrounded by a moat, probably backed by a wooden palisade. Beyond the palisade were many other smaller quarters and hamlets outside the inner town: to the north was the Upper Village and the Jáma, the Widem near the church, Česká Street led up to the Kopeček, and at its foot lay Kamenný řádek. To the southeast of the Valtické quarter lay the Nové Sady, and on the western slope of the Chateau Hill was the Za hradem quarter, later the Jewish Quarter.

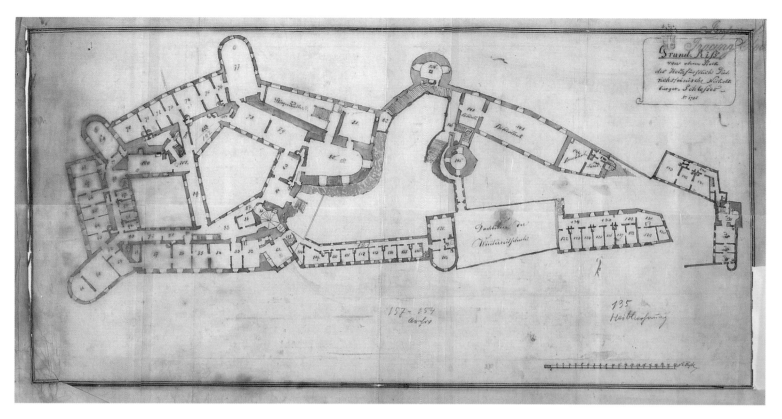

• This 1785 plan of the first floor of the chateau captures the state of the building after the Baroque renovation. Remaining from the Gothic castle were the 15th-century square tower on the chateau's north side, and the 13th-cent. Edge Tower on the second courtyard. Of the former southern castle there remained the original mass of the wall of the four-sided palace in the Hall of Ancestors (13th cent.), the main tower (13th cent.), chapel (14th cent.), and the Rocky Gate below the hall (13th cent.). Also of Gothic style are the well in the courtyard, and the eastern tract with the rectangular tower (15th cent.). At the beginning of the 16th century, defensive bastions were built on the castle courtyards and the Smoke Tower.

The Cardinal rebuilt the south castle as a residential palace. Another tract with a large hall was built alongside it, serving originally as a theater.

The final layout was the result of Baroque reconstruction, in which the northern outer courtyard was built up with a large hall, a riding hall, and apartments for officials. A part of the reconstruction was the eastern terrace supported by an arcade, lightening the compact mass of the chateau.

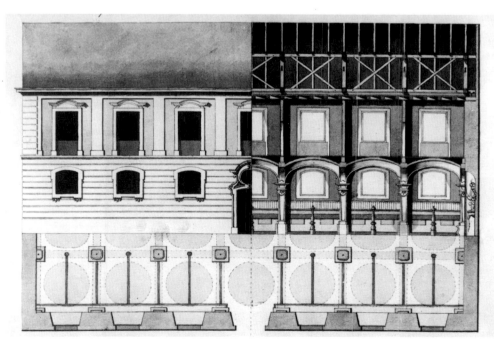

• The facade, cross-section, and floor plan of this building by František Antonín Grimm are part of plans for a stable built in 1743 on the northern courtyard. Today it serves as the foyer to a multipurpose hall.

• The sala terrena, which retains some of its Baroque decoration, was built in 1721-1723 together with the adjacent south terrace. It served as a cool refuge in the summer, and was connected with the park by a stairway near the southwest bastion. The author of the trompe l'oeil wall decoration is Jiří Werle, who also painted the entrance hall.

• The Throne Room. Its luxurious furnishings, throne, and Flemish tapestries created a dignified reception hall worthy of crowned heads of state. Here Maria Theresa met with the Moravian nobility; here Napoleon Bonaparte dictated terms after the Battle of Austerlitz, as did Bismarck after the Battle of Hradec Králové.

A portal on the south courtyard, with sculpture by Ignáce Lengela-chera and wrought ironwork by Heinrich Gottfried Förster.

• At the end of the 17th century a fountain was built in the center of the square. The pedestal carries an allegorical female figure with shield and the Dietrichstein herald with a horn of plenty. The calm pose of this statue of Pomona seems the antithesis of Langelacher's Baroque expressionism in the statues of the Holy Trinity. The author of this statue was probably Ferdinand Gross, whose Marian column stands in the inner courtyard of the castle.

• Sculptor Ignác Lengelacher was brought to Mikulov by Walter Dietrichstein, who undertook the renovation of the burned-out chateau. Legelacher's first task was sculpture on the stairway of the entrance hall. In 1732 on the south courtyard he finished the painted portal with its Atlases, allegorical female figures, and cherubs. In 1726 he decorated the main courtyard with statues of deer and children, vases placed on the gate to the park, and on the rocky gate a cartouche with the insignia of the Dietrichstein-Proskov family.

In town near the Piarist church he placed, at his own expense, a statue of St. Jan Nepomucký. At the provost church he made sculptures for the side altars, and on the entrance gate placed statues of St. Jan Nepomucký and St. Francis Xavier. He decorated the interior of the synagogue, and produced sculptures for the altar of the Capuchin church.

This monumental allegory of the Holy Trinity was created by Lengelacher in 1724 from a design by Antonín Josef Prener. It consists of a three-part pedestal carrying three Toscan columns, and is crowned with a thin, three-sided obelisk. On the volutes of the wings of the pedestal are three angels, symbolizing Faith, Hope, and Love. At the bottom are reliefs of angels with grapes, a cartouche with the Dietrichstein heralds, and a relief depicting the town. Before the columns Langelacher placed statues of St. Jan Nepomucký, St. Francis Xavier, and St. Charles Boromejský, protector from the plague. In the center between the sculptures is a sculpture of Mary with the infant Jesus. The scene is enlivened with cherubs around the statues of Christ and God the Father. The obelisk is crowned by a halo and the dove of the Holy Spirit.

Prospectus arcis et palatii Principis a Dietrichstein Nicolaiburgi.

Profpect des Fürfftich Dietrichfteinifchen Residenz Schloffes zu Nicolspurg.

• This etching, after a drawing by Friedrich Bernard Werner in the period before 1740, captures the Dietrichstein residence before the Baroque reconstruction. The eastern tract of the chateau has been given a large terrace supported by the pillars of an arcade. Below at the level of the park is an orangery, which was torn down in 1830. The gate to the main courtyard is adorned with sculptures by Lengelacher.

• One of the artists employed in the 1720's at the chateau was Brno ironwright Heinrich Gottfried Förster. This master of Baroque ornamentation designed and produced several large and small works of metal to accompany the sculptures of Legelacher. Förster's great bars dominate the entrance from the Main Courtyard to the park, and complement Lengelacher's imposing works. The portal of the southern courtyard with Lengelacher's atlantas, and allegories of Day and Night, are adorned with Förster's window bars. The chateau's entrance hall, closed off by double gates, with excellent examples of wrought-iron vegetation, lead to a stairway, where wrought iron fillers and small stone sculptures show the works of these two Baroque masters together in harmony.

61)

• The theater built by Cardinal Dietrichstein was changed to a library at the beginning of the 18th century. Its shelves hold thousands of volumes, making it one of the most important family libraries in Moravia. The original collection of books, assembled by Adam and Franz Dietrichstein, was removed in 1645 to Sweden, then ransomed for the Renaissance library of Hofman von Grünpichl, regarded as a treasury of 16th century knowledge. Later it was enriched with the Piarist library of Kassian Halaška and the personal library of the Dietrichsteins. The central showcases hold Marie Krystýna's collection of minerals.

• In the late 18th century, South Moravia was a unique Central European cultural area. There were intense intellectual currents, concentrated around the central figures of educated aristocrats, with Josefian and Enlightenment culture mixing with social changes. The Dietrichstein was among the highest nobility in Austria; its seat, Mikulov, was one of three centers of the early Enlightenment in Moravia, along with Brno and Kroměříž. At the Vienna court of Josef II, the Emperor's High Equerry Jan Karel Dietrichstein met and married the enticing Countess Marie Krystýna of Thun, mistress of Josef II and handmaiden to Marie Elisabeth, one of the daughters of Maria Theresa. While Jan Karel served Josef II at the court in Vienna, and in the diplomatic service in Denmark and England, Marie Krystýna took on the management of the Dietrichstein estates. Her efforts, directed by officials of the Dietrichsteins' Enlightenment circle, were carried out in the spirit of new knowledge in the field of natural science. Robota, or unpaid labor required of serfs by their masters, was replaced by wages, and new crops such as maize and potatoes were introduced. The many interests of this many-sided woman are documented by the report that, in 1784 shortly after experiments were carried out at the Prater in Vienna, a hot-air balloon went up, supposedly sewn by the Princess herself.

Marie Krystýna is buried in the family tomb in Mikulov, the town on which she made such an imprint in the 18th century.

• Josef Žabský (1701-1770) was the administrator of the Mikulov estate during the time of Marie Krystýna. After issuance of a decree in 1738 that allowed the state to intervene in relations between peasants and nobles, the estate's operations were reorganized under his direction. Žabský's portrait is the work of Josef Franz Adolf (1685-1762).